My State

MINNESOTA

By Christina Earley

TABLE OF CONTENTS

A Crabtree Seedlings Book

Crabtree Publishing
crabtreebooks.com

School-to-Home Support for Caregivers and Teachers

This book helps children grow by letting them practice reading. Here are a few guiding questions to help the reader build his or her comprehension skills. Possible answers appear in red.

Before Reading:

- What do I know about Minnesota?
    - *I know that Minnesota is a state.*
    - *I know that Minnesota gets very cold in the winter.*
- What do I want to learn about Minnesota?
    - *I want to learn which famous people were born in Minnesota.*
    - *I want to learn what the state flag looks like.*

During Reading:

- What have I learned so far?
    - *I have learned that Saint Paul is the state capital of Minnesota.*
    - *I have learned that Minnesota has 11,842 lakes.*
- I wonder why...
    - *I wonder why the state flower is the showy lady's slipper.*
    - *I wonder why you can sometimes see the northern lights at Voyageurs National Park.*

After Reading:

- What did I learn about Minnesota?
    - *I have learned that you can ride roller coasters at the Mall of America.*
    - *I have learned that the state bird is the loon.*
- Read the book again and look for the glossary words.
    - *I see the word* ***capital*** *on page 6, and the word* ***houseboat*** *on page 14. The other glossary words are found on pages 22 and 23.*

MINNESOTA

Hi! My name is Carter. Welcome to Minnesota!

I live in Bemidji. The Mississippi River starts here.

My city is known as the birthplace of Paul Bunyan.

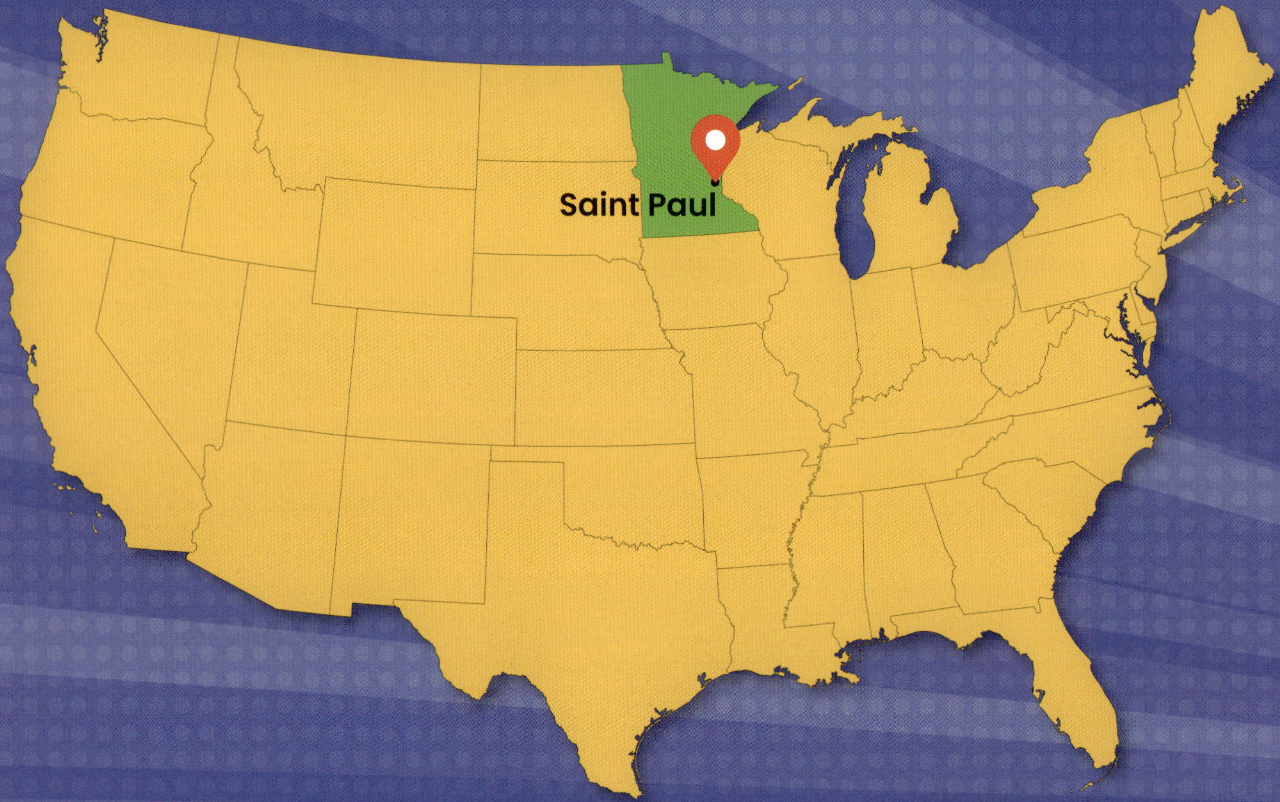

Minnesota is in the **midwestern** United States. The **capital** is Saint Paul.

Fun Fact: Minneapolis is the largest city in Minnesota.

The state bird is the loon.

The showy lady’s slipper is the state flower.

We grow a lot of corn in Minnesota. Some of it is used to make popcorn.

Fun Fact: Minnesota grows more than 1 billion bushels of corn a year.

My state flag is blue. The state **seal** is in the middle.

My family likes to watch the Minnesota Vikings play football.

My family and I stay on a **houseboat** at Voyageurs National Park. Sometimes we see the **northern lights**.

Fun Fact: Minnesota has 11,842 lakes.

I like to look at the sculptures at the Minneapolis Sculpture Garden. The spoon with a cherry is my favorite.

I can see Lake Superior when I ski at Lutsen Mountains.

Singer Prince was born in Minnesota. Football coach John Madden was also born in Minnesota.

Fun Fact: Vice President Walter Mondale was born in Ceylon, Minnesota.

nickelodeon
UNIVERSE
My family and I ride the roller coasters at the Mall of America.

The Runestone **Museum** has a stone said to have been carved by Vikings.

Glossary

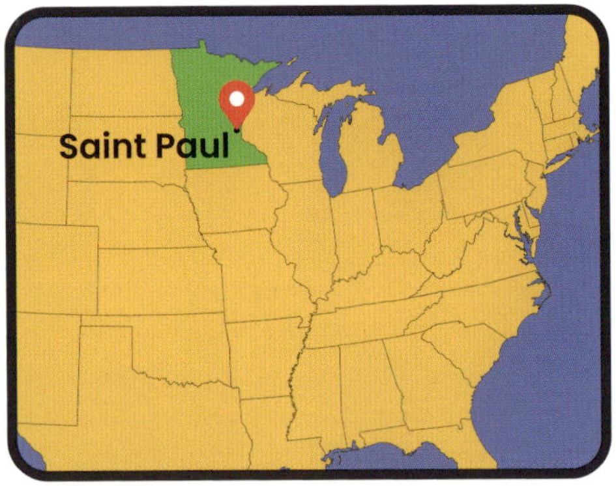

capital (cap-ih-tuhl): The city or town where the government of a country, state, or province is located

houseboat (hows-boat): A boat that is also used as a house

midwestern (mid-west-urn): The northern central part of the United States

museum (mew-zee-uhm): A place where interesting and valuable things are collected for people to see

northern lights (nawr-thern lahyts): Brightly colored lights that sometimes appear in the night sky in Earth's far northern regions

seal (seel): A special design that is used on important papers and other items

Index

About the Author

Christina Earley lives in sunny South Florida with her husband and son. She enjoys traveling around the United States and learning about different historical places. Her hobbies include hiking, yoga, and baking.

Written by: Christina Earley
Designed and Illustrated by: Bobbie Houser
Series Development: James Earley
Proofreader: Melissa Boyce
Educational Consultant: Marie Lemke M.Ed.

Photographs:
Alamy: Pictorial Press Ltd: p. 18 left
Newscom: Kirsten Schmitt/Cal Sport Media: p. 13
Shutterstock: MH Anderson Photography: cover; Dan Thornberg: p. 3; Edgar Lee Espe: p. 4-5, 9; Volina: p. 6, 22; photo.ua: p. 7; Rejean Aline Bedard: p. 8; Serg64: p. 10-11; Fotokostic: p. 11; railway fx: p. 12, 23; Carlos Lucio: p. 14; BlueBarronPhoto: p. 14-15, 22, 23; Checubus: p. 16; Life Atlas Photography: p. 17; Everett Collection: p. 18 right; esperanza casso: p. 20; James Kirkikis: p. 21, 23
whitehouse.gov: p. 19

Crabtree Publishing

crabtreebooks.com 800-387-7650

Printed in the U.S.A./072023/CG20230214

Published in Canada
Crabtree Publishing
616 Welland Avenue
St. Catharines, Ontario
L2M 5V6

Published in the United States
Crabtree Publishing
347 Fifth Avenue
Suite 1402-145
New York, New York, 10016

Library and Archives Canada Cataloguing in Publication
Available at Library and Archives Canada

Library of Congress Cataloging-in-Publication Data
Available at the Library of Congress

Hardcover: 978-1-0398-0520-0
Paperback: 978-1-0398-0552-1
Ebook (pdf): 978-1-0398-0616-0
Epub: 978-1-0398-0584-2